CHECKERBOARD BIOGRAPHY LIBRARY

U.S. PRESIDENTS

The
United States Presidents

WOODROW WILSON

ABDO Publishing Company

BreAnn Rumsch

visit us at
www.abdopublishing.com

Published by ABDO Publishing Company, 8000 West 78th Street, Edina, Minnesota 55439.
Copyright © 2009 by Abdo Consulting Group, Inc. International copyrights reserved in all
countries. No part of this book may be reproduced in any form without written permission from the
publisher. The Checkerboard Library™ is a trademark and logo of ABDO Publishing Company.

Printed in the United States.

Cover Photo: Getty Images
Interior Photos: Alamy pp. 11, 13; AP Images pp. 9, 14, 21, 27, 29; Corbis pp. 10, 18, 19; Getty
    Images pp. 16, 22; iStockphoto p. 32; Library of Congress pp. 5, 12, 15, 17, 23, 25; National
    Archives pp. 20, 24

Editor: Heidi M.D. Elston
Art Direction & Cover Design: Neil Klinepier
Interior Design: Neil Klinepier

Library of Congress Cataloging-in-Publication Data

Rumsch, BreAnn, 1981-
  Woodrow Wilson / BreAnn Rumsch.
     p. cm. -- (The United States presidents)
  Includes index.
  ISBN 978-1-60453-480-1
  1. Wilson, Woodrow, 1856-1924--Juvenile literature. 2. Presidents--United States--Biography--
Juvenile literature. I. Title.

  E767.R94 2009
  973.913092--dc22
  [B]
                                2008025822

CONTENTS

WOODROW WILSON

Woodrow Wilson was the twenty-eighth president of the United States. His honest, fair leadership made him one of America's greatest presidents.

As a student, Wilson studied history and government. After college, he worked as a lawyer and a writer. He also became a college professor.

Wilson's leadership skills soon began to show. He became president of Princeton University. Then, he served as governor of New Jersey. In 1912, he was elected president of the United States.

President Wilson served two terms. During this time, he created many new laws to help Americans. Wilson led the nation through **World War I**. He also wrote a peace plan that earned praise from world leaders.

After Wilson left the White House, he led a quiet life. He spent time with his family and friends. Woodrow Wilson died in 1924.

TIMELINE

1856 - On December 28, Thomas Woodrow Wilson was born in Staunton, Virginia.

1879 - Wilson graduated from the College of New Jersey.

1885 - On June 24, Wilson married Ellen Louise Axson; Wilson wrote his first book, *Congressional Government*.

1886 - Wilson graduated from Johns Hopkins University.

1889 - Wilson published a textbook called *The State*.

1902 - Wilson was elected president of Princeton University.

1910 - Wilson was elected governor of New Jersey.

1913 - On March 4, Wilson became the twenty-eighth U.S. president.

1914 - World War I began in July; Ellen Wilson died on August 6.

1915 - Germany sank the passenger ship *Lusitania*; Wilson married Edith Bolling Galt on December 15.

1916 - Wilson was reelected president.

1917 - On April 2, Wilson asked Congress to declare war on Germany; the United States entered World War I four days later.

1918 - Wilson wrote the Fourteen Points speech; Germany signed an armistice on November 11.

1919 - Wilson joined world leaders in France and signed the Treaty of Versailles on June 28.

1920 - Wilson received the Nobel Peace Prize for founding the League of Nations.

1924 - On February 3, Woodrow Wilson died in Washington, D.C.

DID YOU KNOW?

Woodrow Wilson is the only U.S. president to have earned a PhD.

President Wilson kept a flock of sheep on the White House lawn. That way he could help raise wool for the war effort.

Wilson was the first president to cross the Atlantic Ocean while in office. He traveled to the Paris Peace Conference on a ship called the *George Washington*.

Wilson was the first president to make a radio broadcast.

President Wilson's image is on the $100,000 bill. However, it is no longer used.

Wilson was the last president to ride to his inauguration in a horse-drawn carriage.

YOUNG TOMMY

Thomas Woodrow Wilson was born in Staunton, Virginia, on December 28, 1856. He was called Tommy for most of his young life.

The Wilsons were a close family. Tommy's father, Joseph Ruggles Wilson, was a Presbyterian minister. Tommy's mother was Janet Woodrow Wilson. She was the daughter of a Presbyterian minister. Tommy had two older sisters, Anne and Marion. He also had a younger brother, Joseph Jr.

When Tommy was one year old, his family moved to Augusta, Georgia. He grew up there during the American **Civil War**. The war closed most Southern schools. Therefore, Tommy did not attend school until he was 13 years old. Before then, his father taught him at home. Reading was difficult for Tommy. So, his father took him to many local

FAST FACTS

BORN - December 28, 1856
WIVES - Ellen Louise Axson (1860–1914),
　　　　　Edith Bolling Galt (1872–1961)
CHILDREN - 3
POLITICAL PARTY - Democrat
AGE AT INAUGURATION - 56
YEARS SERVED - 1913–1921
VICE PRESIDENT - Thomas R. Marshall
DIED - February 3, 1924, age 67

8

Tommy's birthplace in Staunton, Virginia

shops and factories. There, Tommy learned to describe everything he saw. At home, Tommy practiced writing and learned to look up words in the dictionary. The Wilsons also read the Bible every day. Tommy eventually overcame his reading problems.

OFF TO COLLEGE

In 1873, Wilson entered Davidson College in North Carolina. He studied there for a year and then left school. However, he spent the next year reading and studying at home.

Wilson returned to college in 1875. He began classes at the College of New Jersey in Princeton, New Jersey. The school later changed its name to Princeton University. While there, Wilson studied public speaking. He also joined a **debate** club. And, he worked on the school's newspaper.

In 1879, Wilson graduated from college. He

Young Wilson

10

was ranked thirty-eighth in a class of 106. After Princeton, Wilson began attending the University of Virginia Law School. Soon, he grew ill and had to quit. Yet he kept studying at home. In 1882, Wilson opened his own law office in Atlanta, Georgia.

The College of New Jersey was officially renamed Princeton University in 1896.

Ellen Louise Axson Wilson

The next year, Wilson traveled to Rome, Georgia, on business. While there, he met Ellen Louise Axson. They became friends and soon fell in love.

Back in Atlanta, Wilson's law business was slow. He realized he did not want to be a lawyer. So, he closed his law office to study to be a college professor.

In 1883, Wilson began taking classes at Johns Hopkins University in Maryland. He studied history and **political science**. In 1885, Wilson wrote his first book. It is called *Congressional Government*. The book earned Wilson great praise. That same year, he and Ellen married on June 24.

Wilson graduated from Johns Hopkins in 1886. Soon after, he dropped the name Thomas. From then on, he called himself Woodrow Wilson.

Gilman Hall was the first major academic building on campus at Johns Hopkins University.

PROFESSOR TO LEADER

The Wilsons moved to Bryn Mawr, Pennsylvania, in 1886. There, Wilson took a job teaching history classes at Bryn Mawr College.

That year, the Wilsons had their first daughter, Margaret. Jessie was born in 1887, and Eleanor followed in 1889. Wilson was a loving father. He liked reading aloud to his daughters. He also enjoyed playing games with them.

In 1888, Wilson became a professor at Wesleyan University in Connecticut. He taught history and **political economy**.

Wilson (front row, third from left) *with the Wesleyan University faculty in 1889*

In addition to teaching, he coached the school's football team. And in 1889, Wilson published a textbook on government called *The State*.

In 1890, Wilson became a law professor at Princeton University. He had great success there. He quickly became the school's most popular teacher. Wilson also wrote many books and articles.

Mr. and Mrs. Wilson (center) *with their three daughters*

In 1902, Princeton elected Wilson as its president. A few years later, he introduced a new way of teaching. It brought teachers and students together in small classes.

Wilson also tried to reorganize the university into smaller colleges. But his plan was defeated. Still, Wilson's leadership at Princeton made him famous.

In 1909, Wilson had problems with the **dean** of the Graduate School. They disagreed on the location of a new graduate college. In the end, the dean gained power over the project. It was a bitter loss for Wilson. He began thinking about a new career.

Because of Wilson's success at Princeton, some people thought he would make a good politician. James Smith Jr. was a powerful member of the **Democratic** Party in New Jersey. He agreed to nominate Wilson for governor.

Wilson accepted the nomination. Smith thought he would be able to direct Wilson's decisions. But Wilson wanted to do the right thing. He did not allow Smith to interfere with his plans. In 1910, Wilson won the election.

While president of Princeton, Wilson and his family lived at Prospect House. The home served as the official presidential residence from 1879 to 1968.

HONEST GOVERNOR

Governor Wilson worked hard for government reforms. He formed a public utility control act. It regulated the prices and services of public utilities, such as transportation systems. He formed an **insurance** system to help injured workers. And he passed new election laws. Wilson also fought for school reforms.

Thomas R. Marshall

Governor Wilson's success earned him national attention. In 1912, the **Democrats** chose him as their presidential candidate. Indiana governor Thomas R. Marshall became Wilson's **running mate**.

While campaigning for president, Wilson traveled around the country.

The **Republican** Party renominated President William Taft and Vice President James S. Sherman. Former president Theodore Roosevelt ran for the **Progressive** Party. Roosevelt's **running mate** was California senator Hiram W. Johnson.

Wilson campaigned hard with his New Freedom program. He promised to reduce **tariffs**, strengthen **antitrust** laws, and reorganize the country's banking system. Voters liked Wilson's ideas. They elected him president.

PRESIDENT WILSON

President Wilson took office on March 4, 1913. He wanted to keep his campaign promises. So, he immediately began working with Congress to pass new laws.

Congress passed the Underwood **Tariff** Act. It reduced tariffs and made goods cheaper for Americans. Reducing tariffs meant the government would make less money. So, Congress approved the Sixteenth **Amendment**. It required Americans to pay an income tax.

Congress passed President Wilson's other New Freedom laws, too. The Federal Reserve Act of 1913 created 12 new government banks. In 1914, the Federal Trade Commission Act and the Clayton **Antitrust** Act were passed. These laws enforced fair business practices.

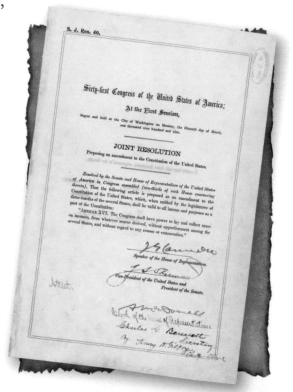

The Sixteenth Amendment explained how the government should tax the population.

PRESIDENT WILSON'S CABINET

FIRST TERM
MARCH 4, 1913– MARCH 4, 1917

- **STATE –** William Jennings Bryan
  Robert Lansing (from June 23, 1915)
- **TREASURY –** William G. McAdoo
- **WAR –** Lindley M. Garrison
  Newton D. Baker (from March 9, 1916)
- **NAVY –** Josephus Daniels
- **ATTORNEY GENERAL –** James C. McReynolds
  Thomas W. Gregory (from September 3, 1914)
- **INTERIOR –** Franklin K. Lane
- **AGRICULTURE –** David F. Houston
- **COMMERCE –** William C. Redfield
- **LABOR –** William B. Wilson

SECOND TERM
MARCH 4, 1917– MARCH 4, 1921

- **STATE –** Robert Lansing
  Bainbridge Colby (from March 23, 1920)
- **TREASURY –** William G. McAdoo
  Carter Glass (from December 16, 1918)
  David F. Houston (from February 2, 1920)
- **WAR –** Newton D. Baker
- **NAVY –** Josephus Daniels
- **ATTORNEY GENERAL –** Thomas W. Gregory
  A. Mitchell Palmer (from March 5, 1919)
- **INTERIOR –** Franklin K. Lane
  John B. Payne (from March 13, 1920)
- **AGRICULTURE –** David F. Houston
  Edwin T. Meredith (from February 2, 1920)
- **COMMERCE –** William C. Redfield
  Joshua W. Alexander (from December 16, 1919)
- **LABOR –** William B. Wilson

Wilson was inaugurated at the U.S. Capitol building in Washington, D.C.

Charles Evans Hughes

Meanwhile, **World War I** started in Europe in July 1914. President Wilson promised to keep the United States out of the war. Soon after the war began, Wilson suffered a personal loss. Ellen Wilson died on August 6. President Wilson was sad and lonely. He had trouble working.

In 1915, Germany sunk a British passenger ship called the *Lusitania*. It killed innocent British and American passengers. The attack angered Americans. But President Wilson stayed calm. He convinced Germany to stop attacking passenger and merchant ships.

Wilson and his second wife, Edith Bolling Galt Wilson

Later that year, Wilson's personal life grew brighter. He met a new friend, Edith Bolling Galt. They married on December 15.

The year 1916 was an election year. President Wilson ran against **Supreme Court justice** Charles Evans Hughes. Hughes's **running mate** was former vice president Charles W. Fairbanks. Voters liked Wilson's new laws. They were also glad he had kept America out of **World War I**. He was reelected to a second term.

WORLD WAR I

During his second term, President Wilson tried to help European leaders end the war. Then, Germany broke its promise not to attack passenger and merchant ships. Great Britain even uncovered a secret German plan. It said Germany intended to start a war between the United States and Mexico.

Germany's actions angered Americans. President Wilson realized he had no choice but to enter the war. On April 2, 1917, he asked Congress to declare war on Germany. Four days later, Congress agreed and the United States entered **World War I**.

The House of Representatives and the Senate agreed to officially declare war on Germany. They passed this joint resolution on April 6, 1917.

When Wilson asked Congress to declare war on Germany,
he said, "The world must be made safe for democracy."

President Wilson traveled around the country speaking about the war. In January 1918, he laid out a peace plan in a speech called Fourteen Points. An important part of the plan was the creation of the League of Nations. This international association would maintain peace among the nations of the world.

In the following months, Germany's military lost major battles. This led German leaders to accept President Wilson's Fourteen Points. Germany signed an **armistice** on November 11, 1918.

Soon after, President Wilson traveled to France. There, he attended the Paris Peace Conference. World leaders signed the Treaty of Versailles on June 28, 1919. The treaty officially ended **World War I**. It also stated the peace plan for Europe after the war.

The treaty did not include all of President Wilson's Fourteen Points. But Wilson made sure it did include the League of Nations. He returned to America with the Treaty of Versailles for Senate approval.

However, many Americans disliked the League of Nations. They did not want to be involved in Europe's problems. So, President Wilson traveled around the nation to promote the League of Nations.

Weary from his travels, Wilson returned to Washington, D.C. There, he had a **stroke** that left him **paralyzed**. He was too weak to fight the Senate. The Senate voted against the Treaty of Versailles because it included the League of Nations.

As Wilson recovered, Congress approved two **amendments** to the **Constitution**. The Eighteenth Amendment passed in 1919. It made buying and selling alcohol illegal. In 1920, the Nineteenth Amendment gave women suffrage, or the right to vote.

Wilson decided not to run in the 1920 election. Later that year, he received the **Nobel Peace Prize**. This award recognized Wilson's work on founding the League of Nations and seeking a fair peace agreement.

In Paris, Wilson (far right) met with *(left to right) Vittorio Orlando of Italy, Lloyd George of Great Britain, and Georges Clemenceau of France. These leaders were known as the Big Four.*

WILSON RETIRES

Wilson retired from the White House in 1921. For the next three years, he led a quiet life in Washington, D.C. Wilson regained some use of his arms and legs. He also formed a law partnership. However, he was too weak to work.

At times, Wilson went to movies and plays. He also liked to listen to books and magazines read aloud to him. Sometimes, he invited friends over for lunch.

On February 3, 1924, Woodrow Wilson died in his sleep. Two days later, he was buried in Washington Cathedral in Washington, D.C. He is the only president buried in the capital city.

Many historians call Wilson one of the greatest U.S. presidents. He worked well with Congress, passing many laws and reforms. Wilson also led America through a troubled time in world history. And he helped end **World War I**.

Wilson never gave up hope that the United States would join the League of Nations. He believed he was right about the League and the peace terms of **World War I**. Today, the League of Nations is considered Wilson's greatest contribution. It led to the creation of the **United Nations**. In it, Woodrow Wilson's vision for world peace lives on.

The Woodrow Wilson House remains the only presidential museum in Washington, D.C. Wilson lived there during his retirement.

OFFICE OF THE PRESIDENT

BRANCHES OF GOVERNMENT

The U.S. government is divided into three branches. They are the executive, legislative, and judicial branches. This division is called a separation of powers. Each branch has some power over the others. This is called a system of checks and balances.

EXECUTIVE BRANCH

The executive branch enforces laws. It is made up of the president, the vice president, and the president's cabinet. The president represents the United States around the world. He or she oversees relations with other countries and signs treaties. The president signs bills into law and appoints officials and federal judges. He or she also leads the military and manages government workers.

LEGISLATIVE BRANCH

The legislative branch makes laws, maintains the military, and regulates trade. It also has the power to declare war. This branch consists of the Senate and the House of Representatives. Together, these two houses make up Congress. Each state has two senators. A state's population determines the number of representatives it has.

JUDICIAL BRANCH

The judicial branch interprets laws. It consists of district courts, courts of appeals, and the Supreme Court. District courts try cases. If a person disagrees with a trial's outcome, he or she may appeal. If the courts of appeals support the ruling, a person may appeal to the Supreme Court. The Supreme Court also makes sure that laws follow the U.S. Constitution.

QUALIFICATIONS FOR OFFICE

To be president, a person must meet three requirements. A candidate must be at least 35 years old and a natural-born U.S. citizen. He or she must also have lived in the United States for at least 14 years.

ELECTORAL COLLEGE

The U.S. presidential election is an indirect election. Voters from each state choose electors to represent them in the Electoral College. The number of electors from each state is based on population. Each elector has one electoral vote. Electors are pledged to cast their vote for the candidate who receives the highest number of popular votes in their state. A candidate must receive the majority of Electoral College votes to win.

TERM OF OFFICE

Each president may be elected to two four-year terms. Sometimes, a president may only be elected once. This happens if he or she served more than two years of the previous president's term.

The presidential election is held on the Tuesday after the first Monday in November. The president is sworn in on January 20 of the following year. At that time, he or she takes the oath of office:

I do solemnly swear (or affirm) that I will faithfully execute the office of President of the United States, and will to the best of my ability, preserve, protect and defend the Constitution of the United States.

LINE OF SUCCESSION

The Presidential Succession Act of 1947 defines who becomes president if the president cannot serve. The vice president is first in the line of succession. Next are the Speaker of the House and the President Pro Tempore of the Senate. If none of these individuals is able to serve, the office falls to the president's cabinet members. They would take office in the order in which each department was created:

Secretary of State

Secretary of the Treasury

Secretary of Defense

Attorney General

Secretary of the Interior

Secretary of Agriculture

Secretary of Commerce

Secretary of Labor

Secretary of Health and Human Services

Secretary of Housing and Urban Development

Secretary of Transportation

Secretary of Energy

Secretary of Education

Secretary of Veterans Affairs

Secretary of Homeland Security

BENEFITS

- While in office, the president receives a salary of $400,000 each year. He or she lives in the White House and has 24-hour Secret Service protection.

- The president may travel on a Boeing 747 jet called Air Force One. The airplane can accommodate 70 passengers. It has kitchens, a dining room, sleeping areas, and a conference room. It also has fully equipped offices with the latest communications systems. Air Force One can fly halfway around the world before needing to refuel. It can even refuel in flight!

- If the president wishes to travel by car, he or she uses Cadillac One. Cadillac One is a Cadillac Deville. It has been modified with heavy armor and communications systems. The president takes Cadillac One along when visiting other countries if secure transportation will be needed.

- The president also travels on a helicopter called Marine One. Like the presidential car, Marine One accompanies the president when traveling abroad if necessary.

- Sometimes, the president needs to get away and relax with family and friends. Camp David is the official presidential retreat. It is located in the cool, wooded mountains in Maryland. The U.S. Navy maintains the retreat, and the U.S. Marine Corps keeps it secure. The camp offers swimming, tennis, golf, and hiking.

- When the president leaves office, he or she receives Secret Service protection for ten more years. He or she also receives a yearly pension of $191,300 and funding for office space, supplies, and staff.

PRESIDENTS AND THEIR TERMS

PRESIDENT	PARTY	TOOK OFFICE	LEFT OFFICE	TERMS SERVED	VICE PRESIDENT
George Washington	None	April 30, 1789	March 4, 1797	Two	John Adams
John Adams	Federalist	March 4, 1797	March 4, 1801	One	Thomas Jefferson
Thomas Jefferson	Democratic-Republican	March 4, 1801	March 4, 1809	Two	Aaron Burr, George Clinton
James Madison	Democratic-Republican	March 4, 1809	March 4, 1817	Two	George Clinton, Elbridge Gerry
James Monroe	Democratic-Republican	March 4, 1817	March 4, 1825	Two	Daniel D. Tompkins
John Quincy Adams	Democratic-Republican	March 4, 1825	March 4, 1829	One	John C. Calhoun
Andrew Jackson	Democrat	March 4, 1829	March 4, 1837	Two	John C. Calhoun, Martin Van Buren
Martin Van Buren	Democrat	March 4, 1837	March 4, 1841	One	Richard M. Johnson
William H. Harrison	Whig	March 4, 1841	April 4, 1841	Died During First Term	John Tyler
John Tyler	Whig	April 6, 1841	March 4, 1845	Completed Harrison's Term	Office Vacant
James K. Polk	Democrat	March 4, 1845	March 4, 1849	One	George M. Dallas
Zachary Taylor	Whig	March 5, 1849	July 9, 1850	Died During First Term	Millard Fillmore

PRESIDENT	PARTY	TOOK OFFICE	LEFT OFFICE	TERMS SERVED	VICE PRESIDENT
Millard Fillmore	Whig	July 10, 1850	March 4, 1853	Completed Taylor's Term	Office Vacant
Franklin Pierce	Democrat	March 4, 1853	March 4, 1857	One	William R.D. King
James Buchanan	Democrat	March 4, 1857	March 4, 1861	One	John C. Breckinridge
Abraham Lincoln	Republican	March 4, 1861	April 15, 1865	Served One Term, Died During Second Term	Hannibal Hamlin, Andrew Johnson
Andrew Johnson	Democrat	April 15, 1865	March 4, 1869	Completed Lincoln's Second Term	Office Vacant
Ulysses S. Grant	Republican	March 4, 1869	March 4, 1877	Two	Schuyler Colfax, Henry Wilson
Rutherford B. Hayes	Republican	March 3, 1877	March 4, 1881	One	William A. Wheeler
James A. Garfield	Republican	March 4, 1881	September 19, 1881	Died During First Term	Chester Arthur
Chester Arthur	Republican	September 20, 1881	March 4, 1885	Completed Garfield's Term	Office Vacant
Grover Cleveland	Democrat	March 4, 1885	March 4, 1889	One	Thomas A. Hendricks
Benjamin Harrison	Republican	March 4, 1889	March 4, 1893	One	Levi P. Morton
Grover Cleveland	Democrat	March 4, 1893	March 4, 1897	One	Adlai E. Stevenson
William McKinley	Republican	March 4, 1897	September 14, 1901	Served One Term, Died During Second Term	Garret A. Hobart, Theodore Roosevelt

PRESIDENT	PARTY	TOOK OFFICE	LEFT OFFICE	TERMS SERVED	VICE PRESIDENT
Theodore Roosevelt	Republican	September 14, 1901	March 4, 1909	Completed McKinley's Second Term, Served One Term	Office Vacant, Charles Fairbanks
William Taft	Republican	March 4, 1909	March 4, 1913	One	James S. Sherman
Woodrow Wilson	Democrat	March 4, 1913	March 4, 1921	Two	Thomas R. Marshall
Warren G. Harding	Republican	March 4, 1921	August 2, 1923	Died During First Term	Calvin Coolidge
Calvin Coolidge	Republican	August 3, 1923	March 4, 1929	Completed Harding's Term, Served One Term	Office Vacant, Charles Dawes
Herbert Hoover	Republican	March 4, 1929	March 4, 1933	One	Charles Curtis
Franklin D. Roosevelt	Democrat	March 4, 1933	April 12, 1945	Served Three Terms, Died During Fourth Term	John Nance Garner, Henry A. Wallace, Harry S. Truman
Harry S. Truman	Democrat	April 12, 1945	January 20, 1953	Completed Roosevelt's Fourth Term, Served One Term	Office Vacant, Alben Barkley
Dwight D. Eisenhower	Republican	January 20, 1953	January 20, 1961	Two	Richard Nixon
John F. Kennedy	Democrat	January 20, 1961	November 22, 1963	Died During First Term	Lyndon B. Johnson
Lyndon B. Johnson	Democrat	November 22, 1963	January 20, 1969	Completed Kennedy's Term, Served One Term	Office Vacant, Hubert H. Humphrey
Richard Nixon	Republican	January 20, 1969	August 9, 1974	Completed First Term, Resigned During Second Term	Spiro T. Agnew, Gerald Ford

PRESIDENT	PARTY	TOOK OFFICE	LEFT OFFICE	TERMS SERVED	VICE PRESIDENT
Gerald Ford	Republican	August 9, 1974	January 20, 1977	Completed Nixon's Second Term	Nelson A. Rockefeller
Jimmy Carter	Democrat	January 20, 1977	January 20, 1981	One	Walter Mondale
Ronald Reagan	Republican	January 20, 1981	January 20, 1989	Two	George H.W. Bush
George H.W. Bush	Republican	January 20, 1989	January 20, 1993	One	Dan Quayle
Bill Clinton	Democrat	January 20, 1993	January 20, 2001	Two	Al Gore
George W. Bush	Republican	January 20, 2001	January 20, 2009	Two	Dick Cheney
Barack Obama	Democrat	January 20, 2009			Joe Biden

"The business of government is to organize the common interest against the special interests." Woodrow Wilson

WRITE TO THE PRESIDENT

You may write to the president at:

**The White House
1600 Pennsylvania Avenue NW
Washington, DC 20500**

You may e-mail the president at:
comments@whitehouse.gov

GLOSSARY

amendment - a change to a country's constitution.

antitrust - relating to laws protecting free trade and fair competition.

armistice - a pause in fighting brought about by an agreement between the two sides.

civil war - a war between groups in the same country. The United States of America and the Confederate States of America fought a civil war from 1861 to 1865.

Constitution - the laws that govern the United States.

dean - a person at a university who is in charge of guiding students.

debate - a contest in which two sides argue for or against something.

Democrat - a member of the Democratic political party. Democrats believe in social change and strong government.

insurance - a contract that helps people pay their bills if they are sick or hurt. People with insurance pay money each month to keep the contract.

justice - a judge on the U.S. Supreme Court.

Nobel Peace Prize - a prize given each year to a person who works hard for world peace.

paralyze - to cause a loss of motion or feeling in a part of the body.

political economy - the study of how a country is governed, taking into consideration both political and economic elements.

political science - the study of government and politics.

Progressive - a member of one of several Progressive political parties organized in the United States. Progressives believed in liberal social, political, and economic reform.

Republican - a member of the Republican political party. Republicans are conservative and believe in small government.

running mate - a candidate running for a lower-rank position on an election ticket, especially the candidate for vice president.

stroke - a sudden loss of consciousness, sensation, and voluntary motion. This attack of paralysis is caused by a rupture to a blood vessel of the brain, often caused by a blood clot.

Supreme Court - the highest, most powerful court in the United States.

tariff - the taxes a government puts on imported or exported goods.

United Nations - a group of nations formed in 1945. Its goals are peace, human rights, security, and social and economic development.

World War I - from 1914 to 1918, fought in Europe. Great Britain, France, Russia, the United States, and their allies were on one side. Germany, Austria-Hungary, and their allies were on the other side. The war began when Archduke Ferdinand of Austria was assassinated. The United States joined the war in 1917 because Germany began attacking ships that weren't involved in the war.

WEB SITES

To learn more about Woodrow Wilson, visit ABDO Publishing Company on the World Wide Web at **www.abdopublishing.com**. Web sites about Woodrow Wilson are featured on our Book Links page. These links are routinely monitored and updated to provide the most current information available.

INDEX